Crafts for Kids Who Are Wild About

Oceans

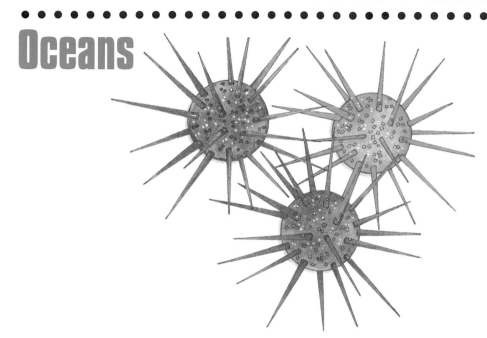

Crafts for Kids Who Are

WILD

ABOUT

OCEANS

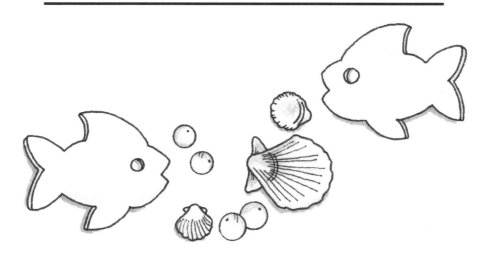

By Kathy Ross
Illustrated by Sharon Lane Holm

The Millbrook Press   Brookfield, Connecticut

For my dear Mom and Dad,
who had some great years by the ocean—K.R.

To Ginny and Steve, who always enjoy
the fun in the surf, sand, and sun—S.L.H.

j602
R720y

Library of Congress Cataloging-in-Publication Data
Ross, Kathy (Katharine Reynolds), 1948–
Crafts for kids who are wild about oceans / Kathy Ross; illustrated by Sharon Lane Holm.
p. cm.
Includes bibliographical references (p.).
Summary: Provides instructions for using common household materials to make fish, sea
urchins, a sea turtle, and other ocean creatures for toys, decoration, or science projects.
ISBN 0-7613-0262-X (lib. bdg.)   ISBN 0-7613-0331-6 (pbk.)
1. Handicraft—Juvenile literature.   2. Marine animals in art—Juvenile literature.
[1. Marine animals in art.   2. Handicraft.]   I. Holm, Sharon Lane, ill. II. Title.
TT160.R714224 1998
745.5—dc21 97–12781 CIP AC

Published by The Millbrook Press, Inc.
2 Old New Milford Road
Brookfield, Connecticut 06804

ct
6/99

Contents

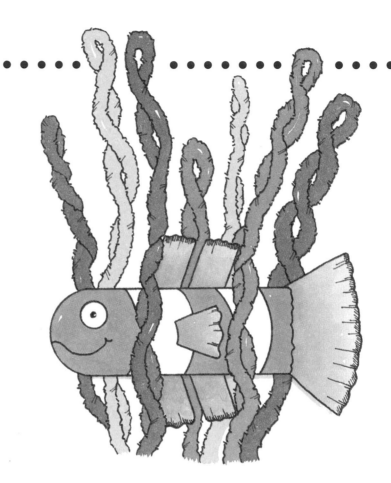

Introduction

Oceans have been called by many the last frontier. Amazing ocean plants and animals are still being discovered and studied for greater understanding. Most of the vast ocean floor has never been viewed by people.

The projects I have included in this book are based on some of the better-known inhabitants of the deep. If you are already WILD about oceans, you will probably know something about these animals. If oceans are a new interest for you, I strongly urge you to go to the library and take out a factual and colorful book about ocean life. This will give you a fuller understanding of the creatures you will be making and greatly increase your enjoyment of them.

Kathy Ross

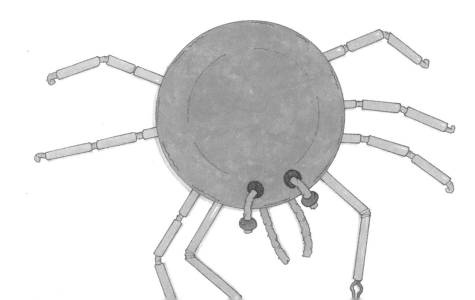

Ocean in a Bag

Here is what you need:

two sturdy zip-to-close bags of the same size
Styrofoam trays in several different colors
white or pastel-colored plastic beads from old jewelry
blue hair gel
small seashells
clear packing tape

Here is what you do:

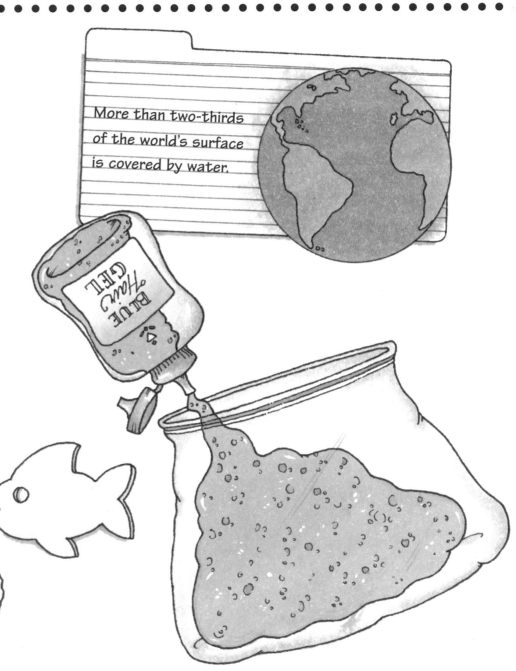

More than two-thirds of the world's surface is covered by water.

Fill one of the bags with blue hair gel so that, when the bag is closed and flattened out, the gel is about ¼ to ½ inch (about 1 cm) thick all over the inside surface of the bag.

Cut 1- to 2-inch (2.5 to 5 cm) -long fish from several different colored Styrofoam trays. (If you can't find colored trays, you can color white ones. Just be sure to use permanent markers.) Put them in the bag. Toss in a few seashells and add some plastic beads for bubbles.

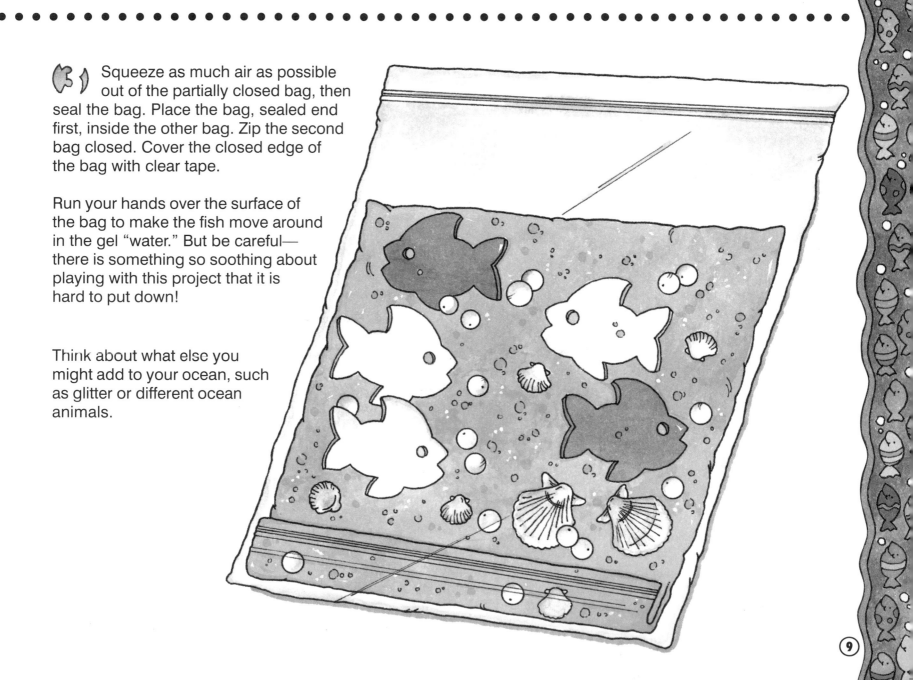

Squeeze as much air as possible out of the partially closed bag, then seal the bag. Place the bag, sealed end first, inside the other bag. Zip the second bag closed. Cover the closed edge of the bag with clear tape.

Run your hands over the surface of the bag to make the fish move around in the gel "water." But be careful—there is something so soothing about playing with this project that it is hard to put down!

Think about what else you might add to your ocean, such as glitter or different ocean animals.

Fish Swimming Through Seaweed Puppet

Here is what you need:

a pair of light-colored adult-size knit gloves
five brightly colored pom-poms
felt scraps
brown or very dark green tissue paper
string
white paper scrap
sharp black marker
hole punch
scissors
white glue
brown poster paint and a paintbrush
Styrofoam tray for drying

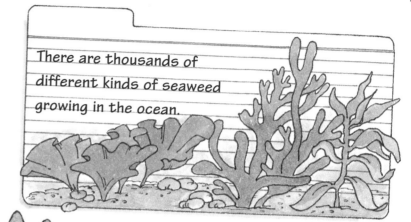

There are thousands of different kinds of seaweed growing in the ocean.

Here is what you do:

1. Paint one of the gloves brown. Let the paint dry.

2. Cut long leaves of seaweed from the tissue paper, and glue them up and down both sides of the painted glove.

3. Turn the five pom-poms into little fish. Cut tails and fins from felt scraps and glue them in place. Punch an eye for each fish from white paper. Draw a pupil on each eye.

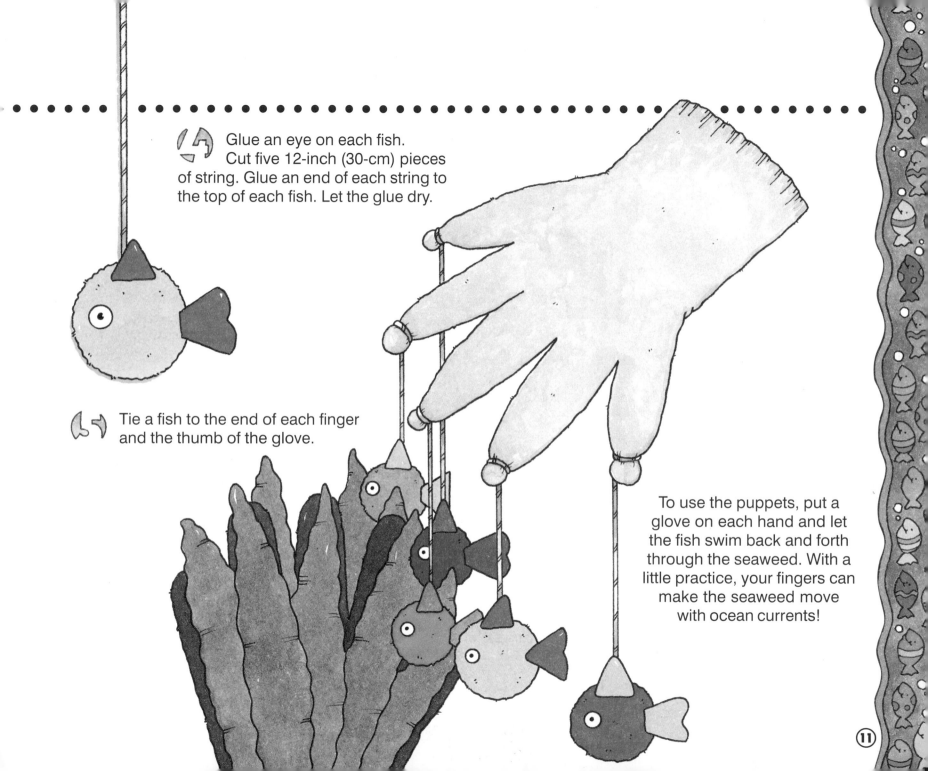

Glue an eye on each fish.
Cut five 12-inch (30-cm) pieces
of string. Glue an end of each string to
the top of each fish. Let the glue dry.

Tie a fish to the end of each finger
and the thumb of the glove.

To use the puppets, put a
glove on each hand and let
the fish swim back and forth
through the seaweed. With a
little practice, your fingers can
make the seaweed move
with ocean currents!

Clam Puppet

Here is what you need:

two 9-inch (23-cm) paper plates
old white sock
gray poster paint and a paintbrush
stapler and staples
two large wiggle eyes
scissors
Styrofoam tray for drying

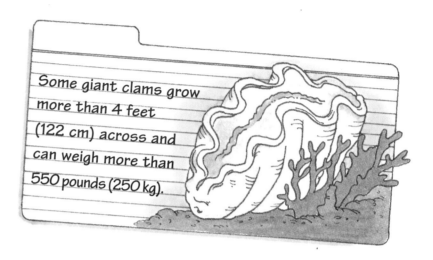

Some giant clams grow more than 4 feet (122 cm) across and can weigh more than 550 pounds (250 kg).

Here is what you do:

Fold a paper plate in half and staple it to keep it folded. Repeat with the second plate.

Place the two folded plates on top of each other to form the top and bottom of a clam-shell. Use the scissors to round off each of the corners of the flat sides of the two plates to make them look more like a shell. Staple the two plates together on each side of the back of the shell.

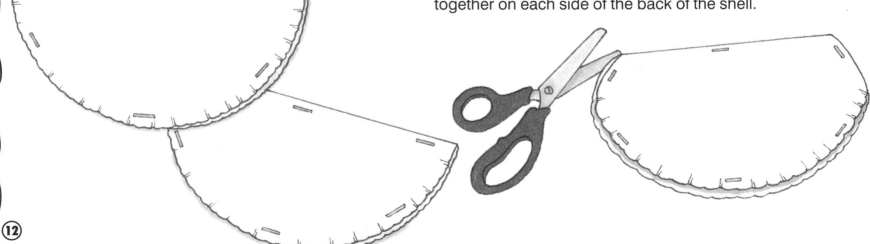

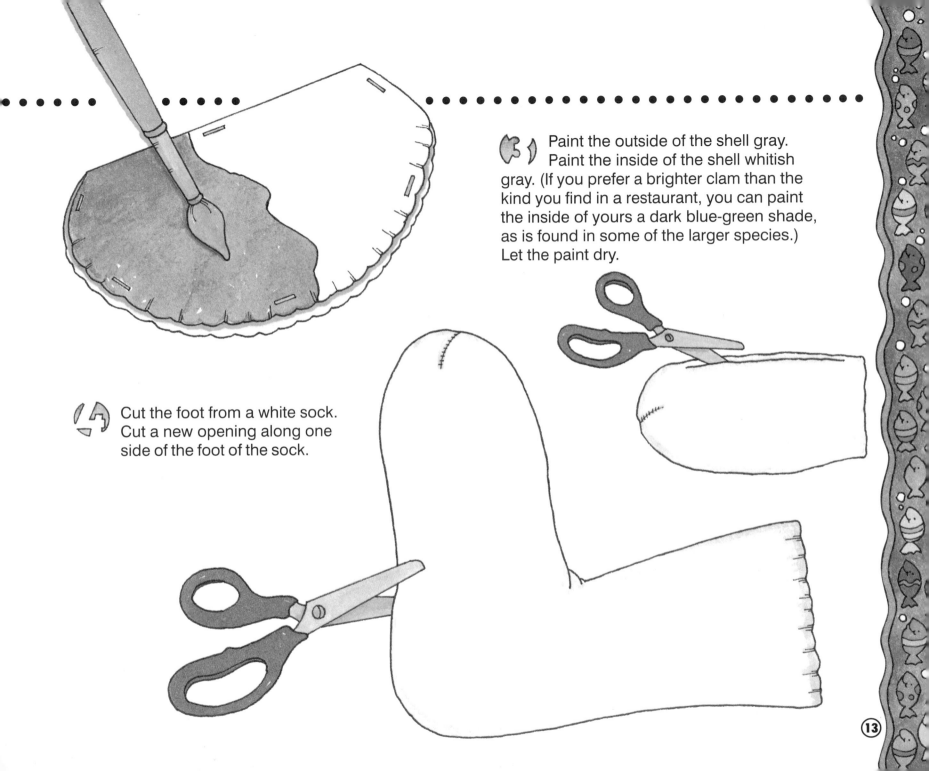

3 Paint the outside of the shell gray. Paint the inside of the shell whitish gray. (If you prefer a brighter clam than the kind you find in a restaurant, you can paint the inside of yours a dark blue-green shade, as is found in some of the larger species.) Let the paint dry.

4 Cut the foot from a white sock. Cut a new opening along one side of the foot of the sock.

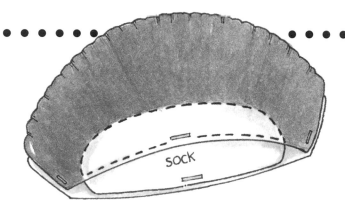

sock

To make the clam inside the shell, staple the top of the cut opening of the sock inside the back part of the top of the shell and staple the bottom cut opening of the sock to the bottom of the shell. Before putting in the final staple, pull any excess sock material together and staple it neatly.

Glue two large wiggle eyes on the clam or make your own eyes from felt or cut paper.

To open and shut the clam, put your thumb on the bottom of the shell and your pinkie on top. Your other fingers go inside the clam so you can make it wiggle when the shell opens.

Pile of Sea Urchins

Here is what you need:

three 2-inch (5-cm) Styrofoam balls
toothpicks
poster paints in three bright colors and a paintbrush
white glue
clear plastic glitter, or salt
margarine tubs and plastic spoons for mixing
Styrofoam tray for drying
newspaper to work on

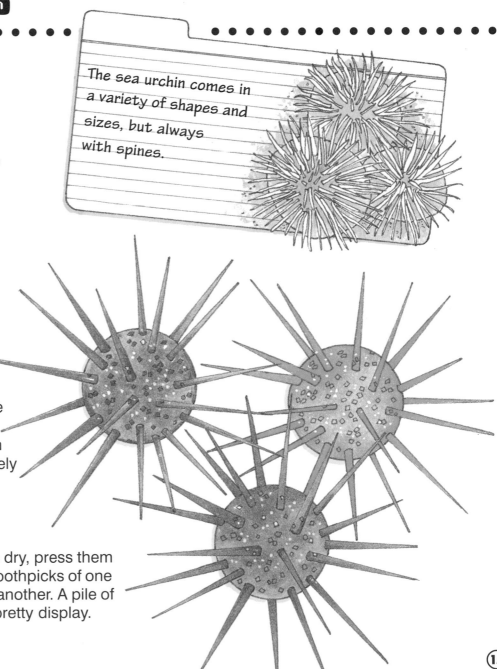

The sea urchin comes in a variety of shapes and sizes, but always with spines.

Here is what you do:

Cover all three Styrofoam balls with toothpicks to make spines on each sea urchin. You can paint your sea urchins fanciful colors, or you can look for pictures of real sea urchins and copy those colors. Mix a small amount of white glue into each color of paint you use. Paint each sea urchin a different color, then immediately sprinkle the wet paint with glitter or salt.

When the sea urchins are dry, press them gently together until the toothpicks of one connect with the body of another. A pile of sea urchins makes a pretty display.

Soft Sculpture Snail

Here is what you need:

pair of old pantyhose
fiberfill
two safety pins
two large wiggle eyes
pipe cleaner
white glue
scissors
poster paint and a paintbrush
Styrofoam tray to work on

Fossil records show that snails have lived in the oceans for more than 500 million years.

Here is what you do:

Cut one leg off the pantyhose. Stuff the leg evenly with fiberfill to about 4 inches (10 cm) from the opening. Hold the edges of the stuffed leg of the pantyhose together and tuck the seam down between the stuffing and the stocking on one side.

Starting at the foot, roll the stuffed leg to make a spiraled snail shell. Use the two safety pins to hold the rolled stocking in place by pinning it to itself on each side of the opening. Rub glue between the folds of the wrapped stocking leg to help hold it in place.

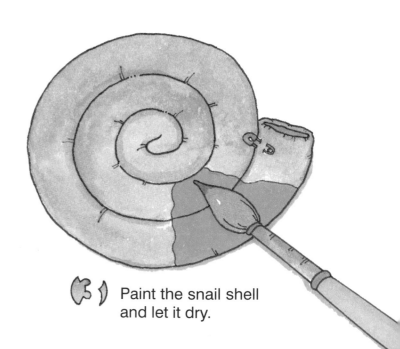

Paint the snail shell and let it dry.

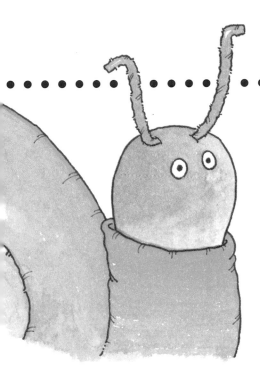

To make the snail head, cut the foot from the second stocking. Stuff half of the foot with fiberfill. Push the unstuffed end of the foot down into the opening of the shell, between the two safety pins, so that the stuffed end sticks out like a head peeking out of a shell. Rub glue around the inner opening of the shell to hold the head in place.

Cut a 6-inch (15-cm) piece of pipe cleaner. Poke one end through one side of the top of the snail head and out the other side to make antennae for the snail. Curl the end of each antenna into a tiny knob.

Glue two wiggle eyes on the front of the snail head.

Maybe you should make a friend for your snail.

Pinching Lobster

Here is what you need:

cardboard paper-towel tube
five cupcake wrappers
blue construction paper
two paper fasteners
red, blue, and green poster paint and a paintbrush
white glue
scissors
hole punch
newspaper to work on
Styrofoam tray for drying

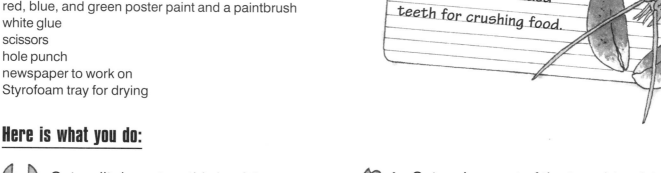

One of the lobster's claws has fine, sharp teeth for catching and holding prey. The other claw has dull, rounded teeth for crushing food.

Here is what you do:

Cut a slit down two-thirds of the cardboard tube. Beginning at the bottom of the slit, cut eight slits, 1 inch (2.5 cm) long and ½ inch (1.25 cm) apart, along each side of the slit edge of the tube.

Fold every other tab in and the tab next to it out to form the eight legs of the lobster.

Cut a piece out of the top side of the slit end of the tube 4 inches (10 cm) long and 1 inch (2.5 cm) wide. Cut a narrow slit down each of the two remaining sides of the tube and fold them back to form antennae for the lobster.

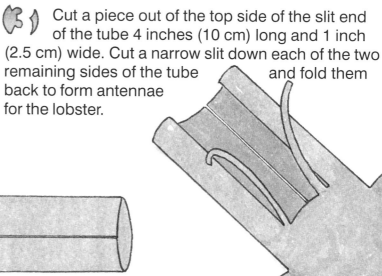

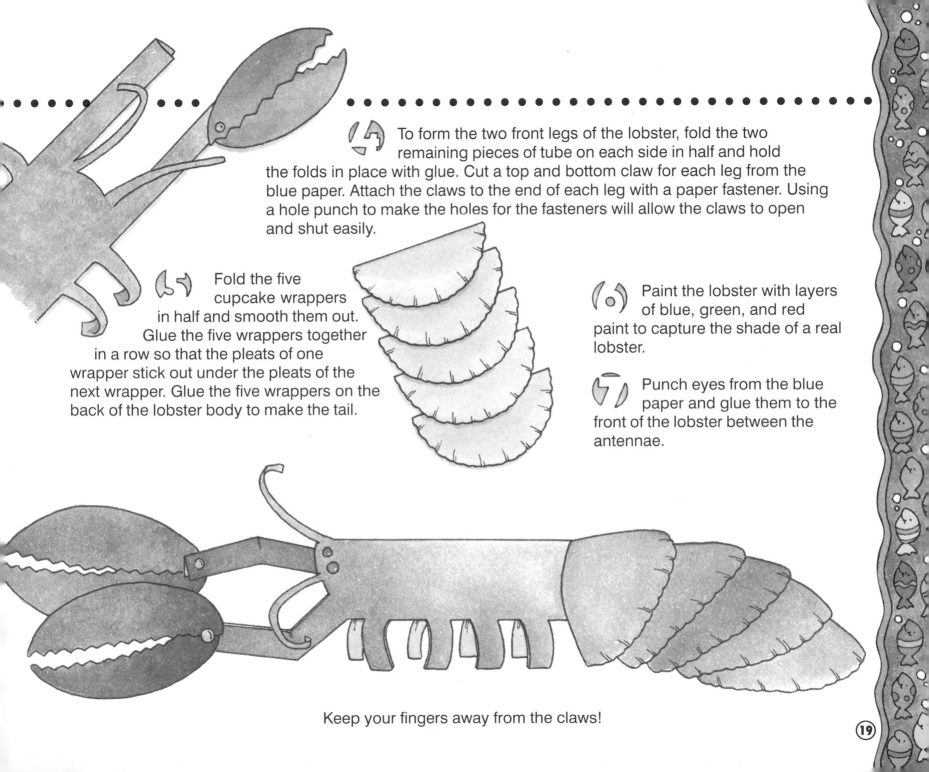

To form the two front legs of the lobster, fold the two remaining pieces of tube on each side in half and hold the folds in place with glue. Cut a top and bottom claw for each leg from the blue paper. Attach the claws to the end of each leg with a paper fastener. Using a hole punch to make the holes for the fasteners will allow the claws to open and shut easily.

Fold the five cupcake wrappers in half and smooth them out. Glue the five wrappers together in a row so that the pleats of one wrapper stick out under the pleats of the next wrapper. Glue the five wrappers on the back of the lobster body to make the tail.

Paint the lobster with layers of blue, green, and red paint to capture the shade of a real lobster.

Punch eyes from the blue paper and glue them to the front of the lobster between the antennae.

Keep your fingers away from the claws!

Crab Puppet

Here is what you need:

6-inch (15-cm) paper bowl
light cardboard
five 12-inch (30-cm) blue or green
  pipe cleaners
two black beads
eight green plastic flexi-straws
two hairpins
blue and green poster paint and
  a paintbrush
pencil
stapler and staples
scissors
newspaper to work on

Here is what you do:

Trace around the opening of the bowl on the light cardboard and cut the circle out.

Use six of the straws and cut 18 pieces, each from 1 to 2 inches (2.5 to 5 cm) long.

Cut four pipe cleaners in half so that you have eight legs for the crab. String three pieces of straw on each of the six legs to form joints. Fold one end of each pipe cleaner to hold the straws on. Staple the other end to one edge of the plate, putting three legs on each side.

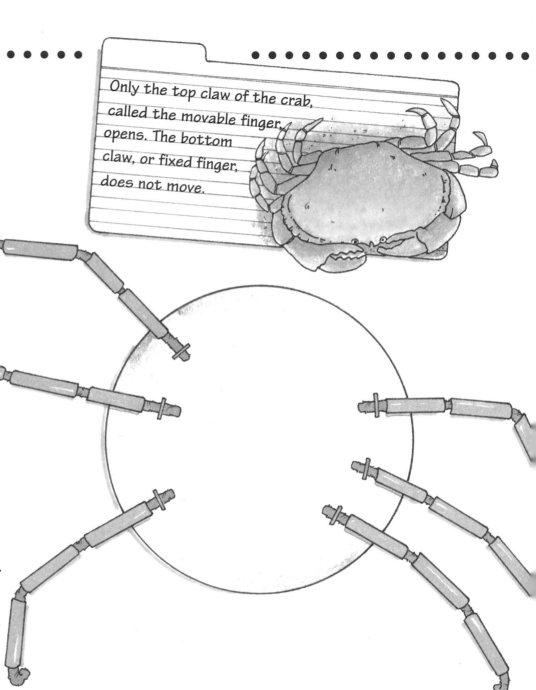

Only the top claw of the crab, called the movable finger, opens. The bottom claw, or fixed finger, does not move.

To make the front legs with claws, cut a 6-inch (15-cm) piece off the top of the two flexi-straws. String a straw onto each of the two remaining pipe cleaner legs. The pipe cleaner should be strung to just past the bend in the straw, leaving the top portion of the straw empty. Push the folded end of a hairpin into the open end of each straw to form the claws. Staple the legs pointing slightly forward at one end and on each side of the crab.

Poke two holes in the edge of the bowl about 1½ inches (4 cm) apart. String a 4-inch (10-cm) piece of pipe cleaner into the bowl through one hole and out through the other. String a bead on the end of each of the pipe cleaners to make the eyes of the crab.

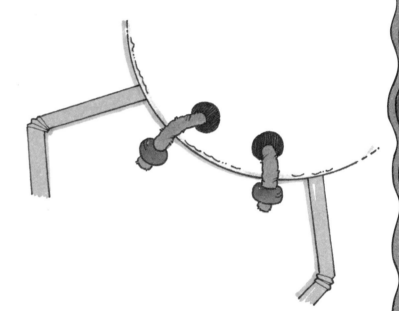

Fold a 5-inch (13-cm) piece of pipe cleaner in half. To form the antennae, staple it to the rim of the bowl between the eyes.

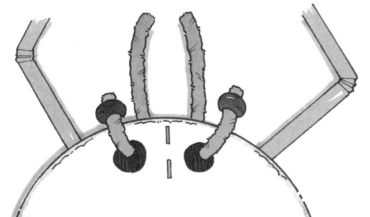

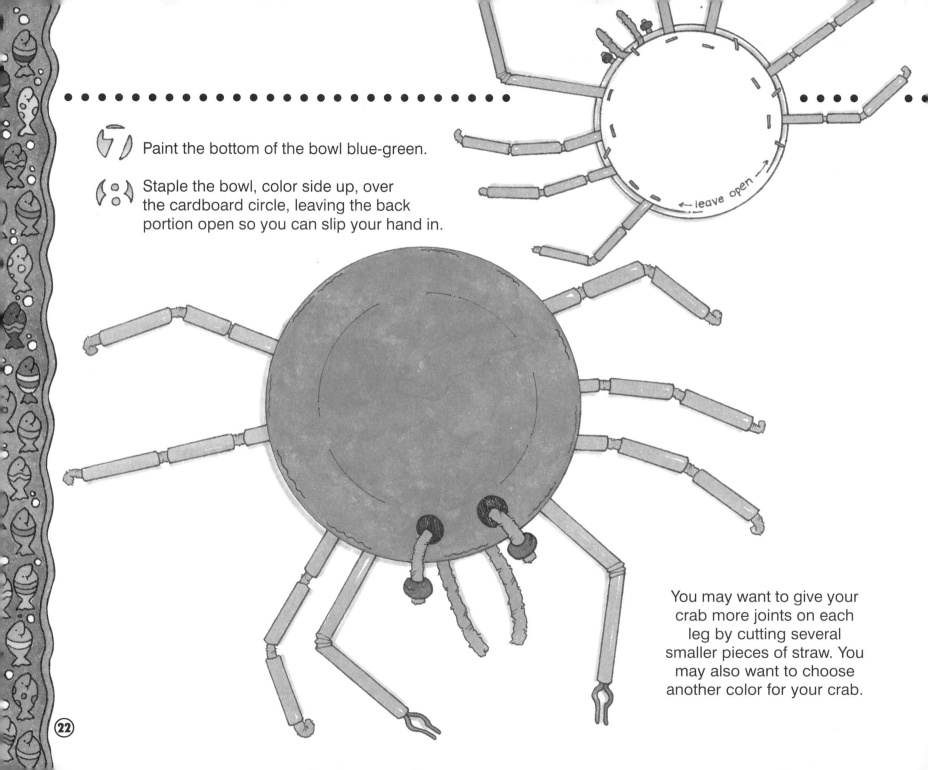

Paint the bottom of the bowl blue-green.

Staple the bowl, color side up, over the cardboard circle, leaving the back portion open so you can slip your hand in.

← leave open

You may want to give your crab more joints on each leg by cutting several smaller pieces of straw. You may also want to choose another color for your crab.

Soft Sculpture Sea Turtle

Here is what you need:

two oval-shaped shoulder pads of similar size
old glove
scissors
white glue
two wiggle eyes

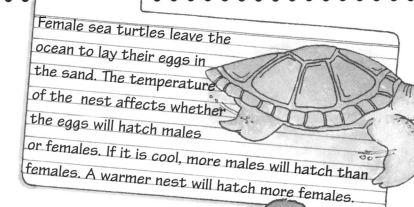

Female sea turtles leave the ocean to lay their eggs in the sand. The temperature of the nest affects whether the eggs will hatch males or females. If it is cool, more males will hatch than females. A warmer nest will hatch more females.

Here is what you do:

Cut the four fingers and the thumb off the glove.

Turn one shoulder pad over so that the top of the pad forms the bottom shell of the turtle. Glue two fingers on the front and back edge of each side of the pad for the legs of the turtle. Glue the glove thumb between the two front legs to form the turtle's head.

Glue the second pad, top up, over the legs and head to form the top shell of the turtle.

Glue two wiggle eyes on the head.

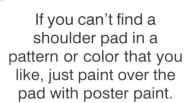

If you can't find a shoulder pad in a pattern or color that you like, just paint over the pad with poster paint.

23

Coral and Seahorse Stabile

Here is what you need:

five 12-inch (30-cm) orange pipe cleaners
construction paper in three bright colors
three 12-inch pipe cleaners, one to match each of the
    three paper colors
plastic lid from laundry detergent bottle
sand
white glue
markers
margarine tub and plastic spoon for mixing

Here is what you do:

1) Fill the plastic lid with sand. Pour the sand into the margarine tub. Add enough glue to the sand to moisten it and hold it together when mixed. Press the gluey sand back in the plastic lid.

2) Cut three pieces of orange pipe cleaner from 7 to 8 inches (18 to 19 cm) long. Wrap smaller pieces of pipe cleaner around them to form the branches of coral. Punch the ends of each of the three large pipe cleaner stems into the wet sand to "plant" them. The sand will harden as it dries and hold the coral in place.

Seahorses use their tails for hanging onto sea plants and coral to keep from being carried away with the currents.

3) Sketch the outline of a seahorse without the tail on one of the pieces of colored paper.

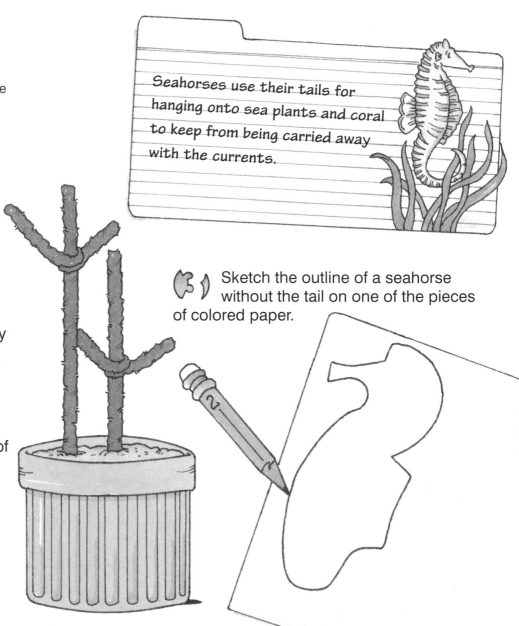

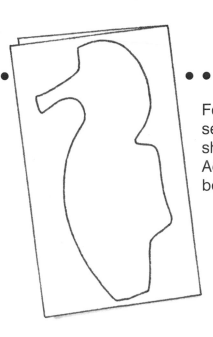

Fold the paper in half and cut out the seahorse so that you end up with two cutout shapes, one for each side of the seahorse. Add details such as an eye and fins to both sides of the seahorse with markers.

Cut a piece of pipe cleaner 3½ inches (9 cm) long and the same color as the paper you used to make the seahorse. Glue the two sides of the seahorse together with the pipe cleaner sticking down out of the bottom for the tail. Make seahorses in three different colors.

Wrap the tail of each seahorse around a branch of the coral.

Make sure your seahorses are holding on tight. They are very weak swimmers and could easily drift away.

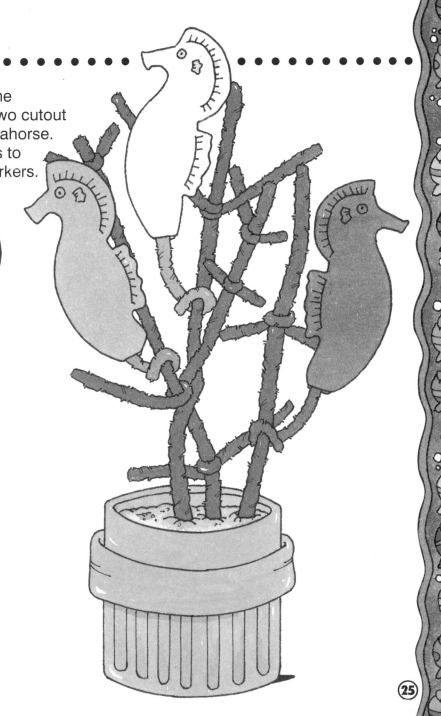

Sea Star

Here is what you need:

light cardboard
pencil
paper fastener
yellow poster paint and paintbrush
white glue
sand
scissors
margarine tub and plastic spoon for mixing
newspaper to work on

If a sea star is unfortunate enough to lose one of its arms, it is able to grow a new one!

Here is what you do:

Draw the shape of a sea star on cardboard. Cut the shape out.

Cut one arm off the sea star. Use it as a pattern to draw a new arm with extra cardboard on it so that it can be attached to the back of the sea star. Cut out the arm.

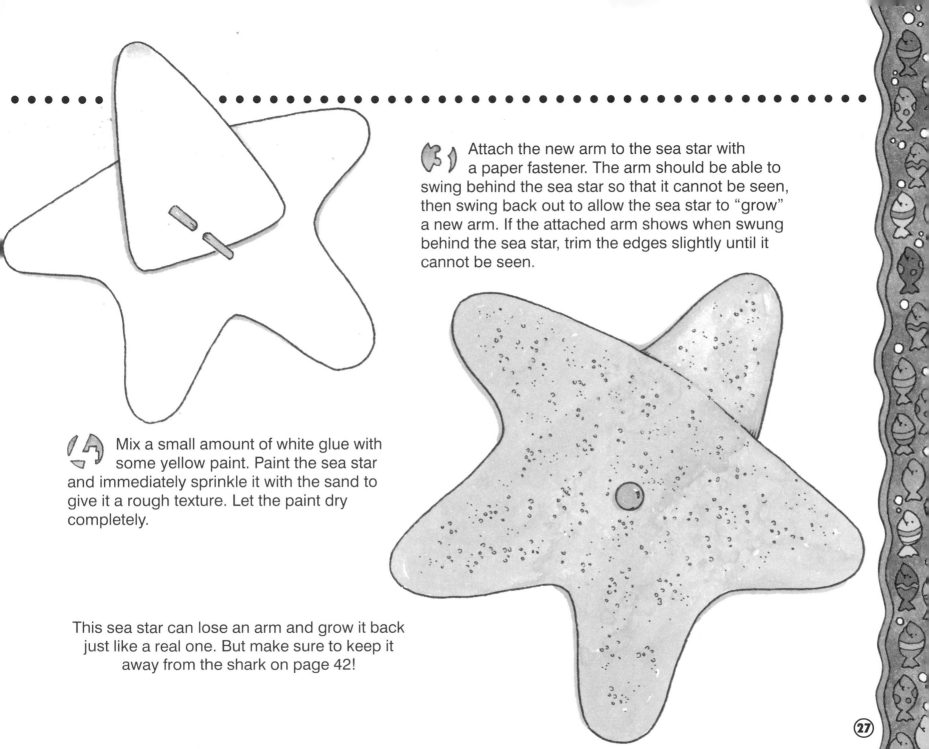

Attach the new arm to the sea star with a paper fastener. The arm should be able to swing behind the sea star so that it cannot be seen, then swing back out to allow the sea star to "grow" a new arm. If the attached arm shows when swung behind the sea star, trim the edges slightly until it cannot be seen.

Mix a small amount of white glue with some yellow paint. Paint the sea star and immediately sprinkle it with the sand to give it a rough texture. Let the paint dry completely.

This sea star can lose an arm and grow it back just like a real one. But make sure to keep it away from the shark on page 42!

Jellyfish Windsock

Here is what you need:

two clear kitchen trash bags
cellophane tape
string
clear Con-tac paper
black marker
sequins
tissue paper in many different colors
stapler and staples
scissors

Here is what you do:

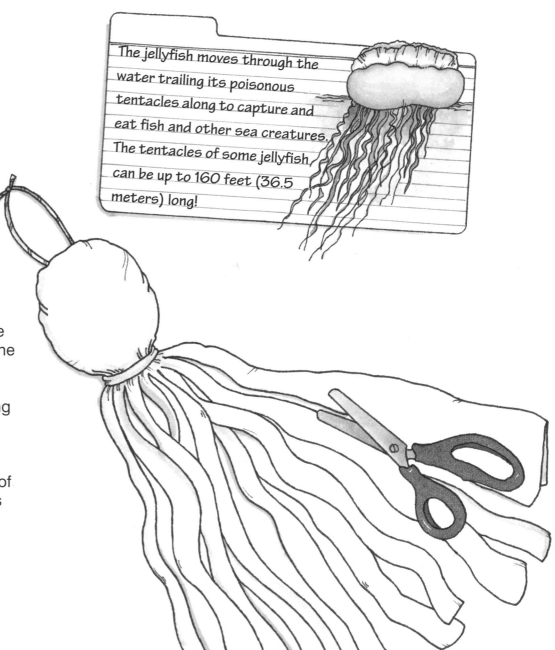

The jellyfish moves through the water trailing its poisonous tentacles along to capture and eat fish and other sea creatures. The tentacles of some jellyfish can be up to 160 feet (36.5 meters) long!

1. Crumple one of the trash bags into a ball and stuff it into the corner of the other bag. The ball will be the head of the jellyfish. Tape around the bottom of the ball to form a neck.

2. Cut part of the trash bag hanging down from the head into long strips to make the tentacles.

3. Push a string through the neck of the jellyfish and tie the two ends together to make a hanger for the windsock.

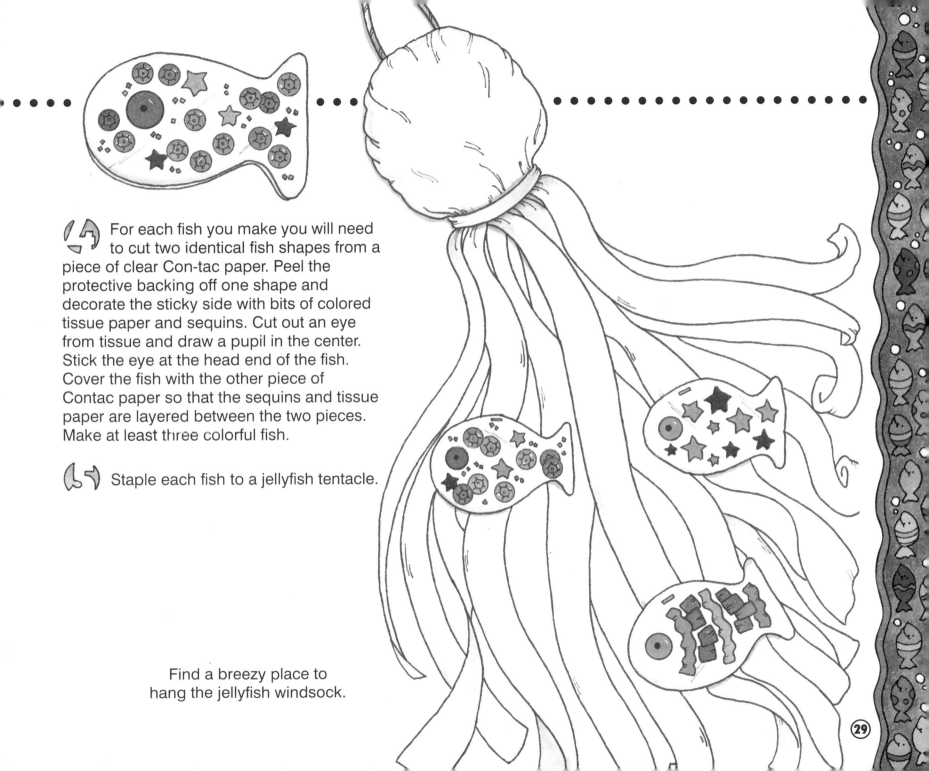

For each fish you make you will need to cut two identical fish shapes from a piece of clear Con-tac paper. Peel the protective backing off one shape and decorate the sticky side with bits of colored tissue paper and sequins. Cut out an eye from tissue and draw a pupil in the center. Stick the eye at the head end of the fish. Cover the fish with the other piece of Contac paper so that the sequins and tissue paper are layered between the two pieces. Make at least three colorful fish.

Staple each fish to a jellyfish tentacle.

Find a breezy place to hang the jellyfish windsock.

Friendly Octopus

Here is what you need:

nine 9-inch (22-cm) paper plates
scissors
white and black construction-paper scraps
hole punch
yarn or string
poster paint and a paintbrush
stapler and staples
white glue
newspaper to work on

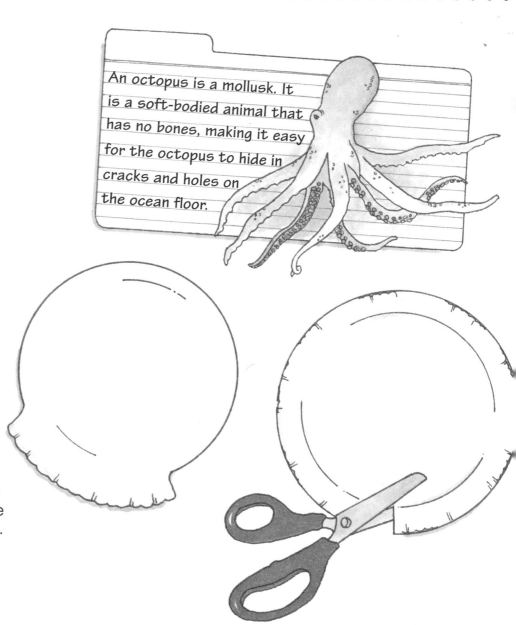

An octopus is a mollusk. It is a soft-bodied animal that has no bones, making it easy for the octopus to hide in cracks and holes on the ocean floor.

Here is what you do:

Cut a round head shape from the center of one paper plate, leaving about 4 inches (10 cm) of the bumpy rim of the plate for the neck.

To make each of the eight legs, cut through the rim of a plate and cut the entire rim off.

Staple all eight legs together, with the legs fanned out. Staple the legs to the back of the neck of the octopus head.

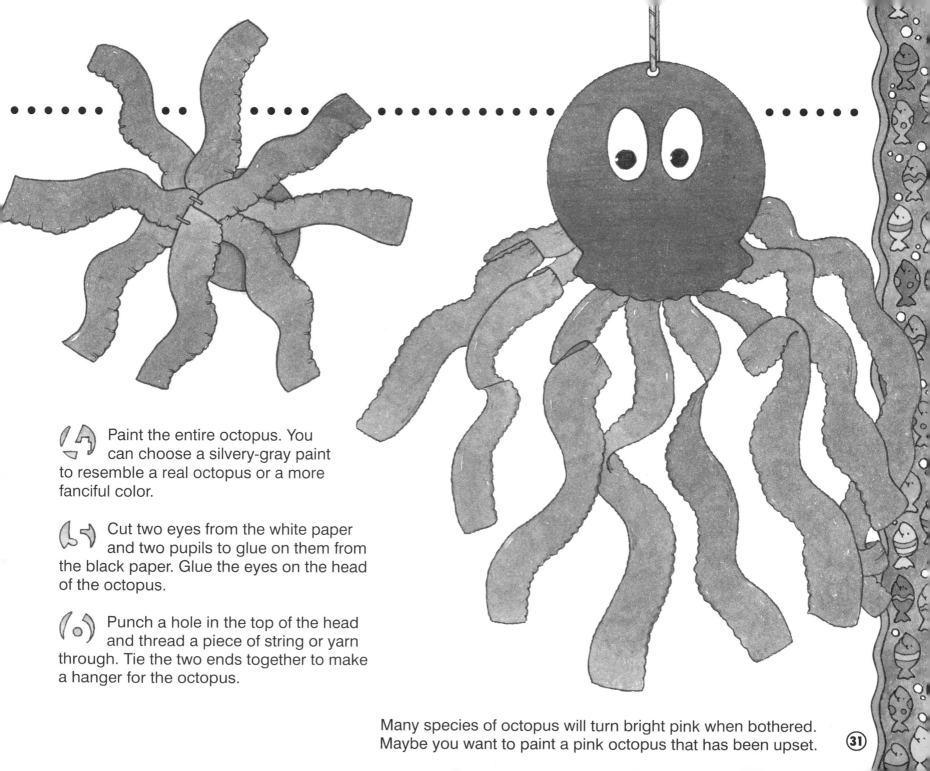

Paint the entire octopus. You can choose a silvery-gray paint to resemble a real octopus or a more fanciful color.

Cut two eyes from the white paper and two pupils to glue on them from the black paper. Glue the eyes on the head of the octopus.

Punch a hole in the top of the head and thread a piece of string or yarn through. Tie the two ends together to make a hanger for the octopus.

Many species of octopus will turn bright pink when bothered. Maybe you want to paint a pink octopus that has been upset.

Slithering Eel

Here is what you need:

spool of green ribbon 1¼ inches (3 cm) wide
pipe cleaners
stapler and staples
white glue
yellow paper scrap
scissors
brown marker
brown poster paint and a paintbrush
newspaper to work on

All European and North American eels return to the Sargasso Sea off Bermuda to mate and lay eggs.

Here is what you do:

Cut two pieces of green ribbon, each 2½ to 3 feet (76 to 91 cm) long.

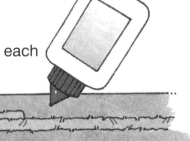

Rub glue over the entire length of one of the ribbons. Run a line of pipe cleaners along the ribbon with the ends of the pipe cleaners overlapping each other.

Put the second ribbon on top of the first so that the pipe cleaners are between the two ribbons. Staple the ribbons together along the two long sides.

Cut one end of the ribbons into a point and staple it closed for the tail of the eel.

Round off and then staple the other end of the ribbons to make the head of the eel.

Turn the ribbons so that one edge is the bottom of the long flat body of the eel. Curve the body back and forth to look like it is slithering. The pipe cleaners will help the ribbon to hold this shape while the glue is drying.

To give your eel the mottled look of a real eel, give it a thin layer of brown paint, allowing the green to show through.

Cut two eyes and two fins from scrap paper. Draw a pupil in the center of each eye with the marker. Glue an eye on each side of the eel's head. Glue a fin on each side of the eel at the head end of the body. Dab the fins with some brown paint.

Remember, eels can become quite aggressive if they are not handled very carefully!

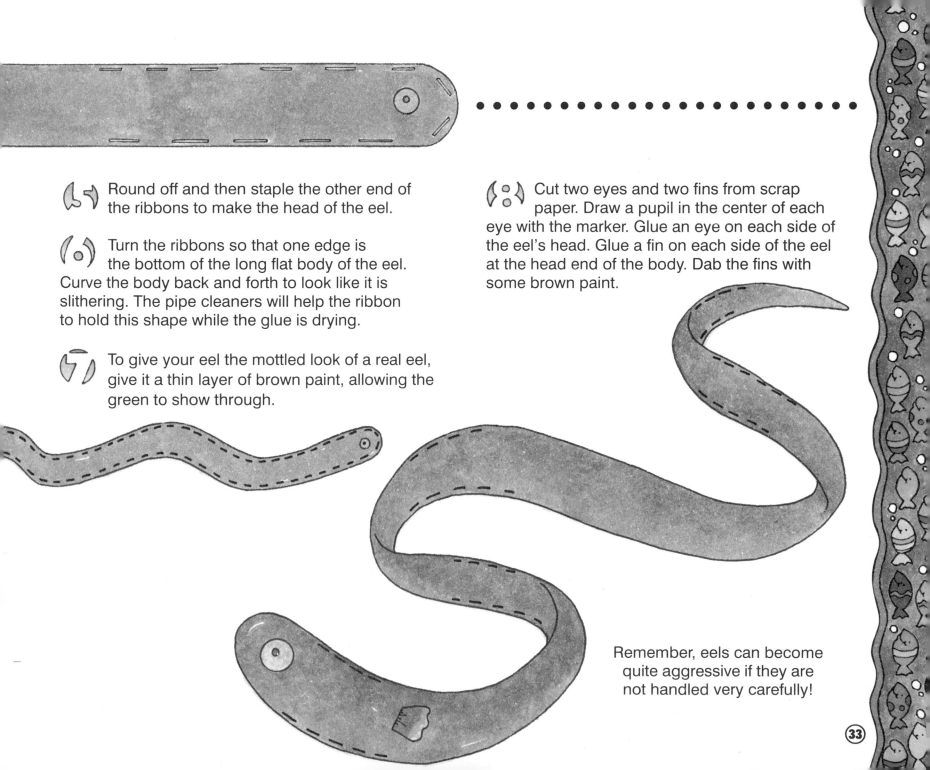

Rippling Ray Puppet

Here is what you need:

four 9-inch (22-cm) paper plates
three paper-towel tubes
two rubber bands
black paper scrap
white glue
gray poster paint and a paintbrush
chopstick
stapler and staples
Styrofoam tray for drying
newspaper to work on

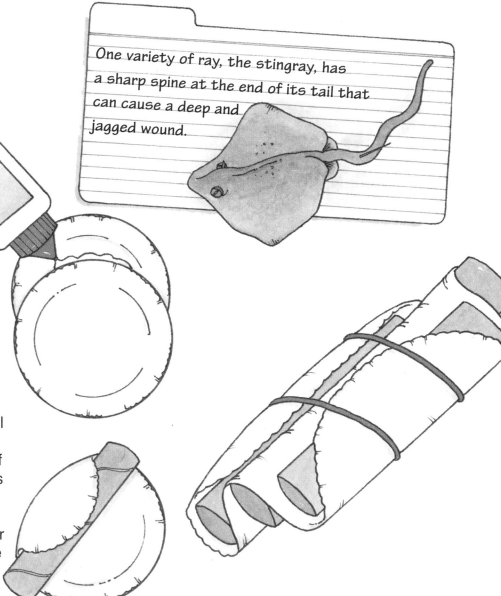

One variety of ray, the stingray, has a sharp spine at the end of its tail that can cause a deep and jagged wound.

Here is what you do:

Cover the top of one paper plate with a thin layer of glue. Cover it with another plate. Glue the other two plates together in the same way.

While the glue is still wet, stack the two sets of plates on top of each other, but don't glue the stacks together. Roll one edge of the plates over a paper-towel tube. Do the same with the opposite edge of the plates. Put another tube under the plates between the two top tubes and shape the plates over it. This will give the plates the rippling effect of a swimming ray. Use rubber bands to hold the tubes in the rippled shape until the glue has dried.

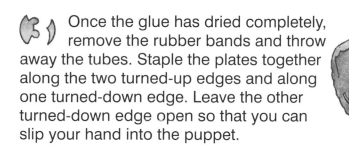

3. Once the glue has dried completely, remove the rubber bands and throw away the tubes. Staple the plates together along the two turned-up edges and along one turned-down edge. Leave the other turned-down edge open so that you can slip your hand into the puppet.

4. Glue the chopstick on the top of the open edge of the puppet with the pointed end more than half off the puppet to form the tail. Let the glue dry before continuing.

5. Paint the ray gray on both sides and let it dry on the Styrofoam tray.

6. Cut two eyes from black paper. Glue them on the top of the closed end of the puppet.

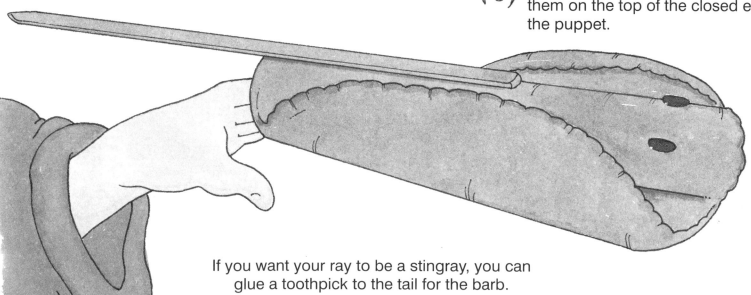

If you want your ray to be a stingray, you can glue a toothpick to the tail for the barb.

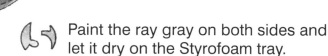

Sea Anemone Stabile

Here is what you need:

about twenty-five 12-inch (30-cm) -long pipe cleaners
poster paint and a paintbrush
baby-food jar lid 3 to 4 inches (7.5 to 10 cm) across
old sock
fiberfill
1½-inch (3.75-cm) Styrofoam ball
white glue
scissors
Styrofoam tray to work on and for drying

Here is what you do:

Ask an adult to cut the Styrofoam ball in half with a knife. Glue the flat side of one half of the ball into the inside of the baby-food jar lid.

Bend each of the pipe cleaners in half and twist them around themselves. Push the loose ends of the pipe cleaners into the base of the Styrofoam ball to make the tentacles of the sea anemone.

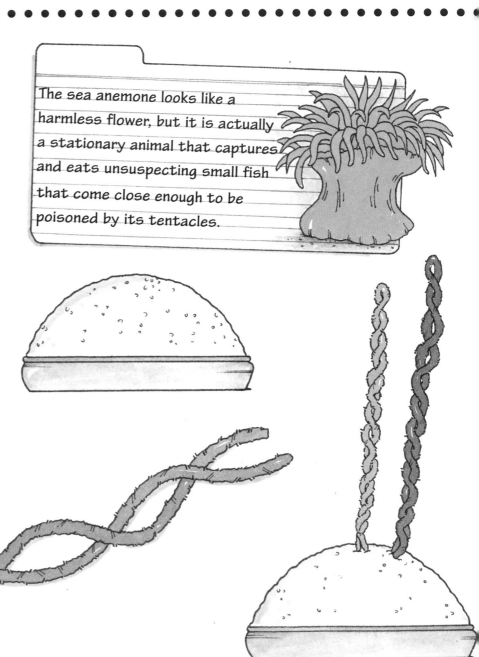

The sea anemone looks like a harmless flower, but it is actually a stationary animal that captures and eats unsuspecting small fish that come close enough to be poisoned by its tentacles.

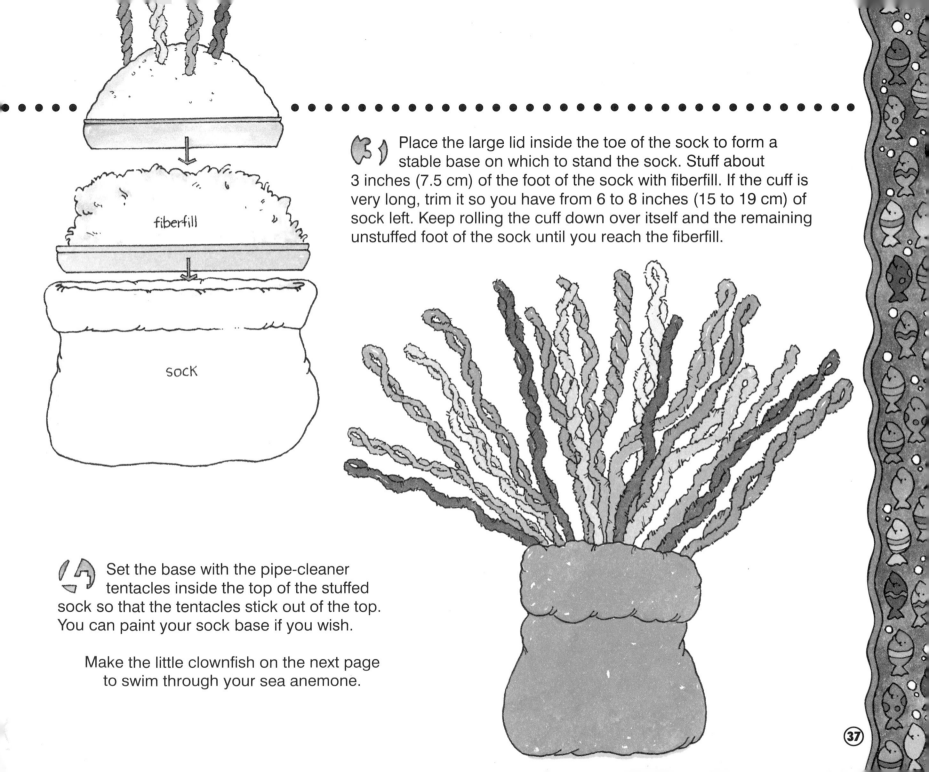

Place the large lid inside the toe of the sock to form a stable base on which to stand the sock. Stuff about 3 inches (7.5 cm) of the foot of the sock with fiberfill. If the cuff is very long, trim it so you have from 6 to 8 inches (15 to 19 cm) of sock left. Keep rolling the cuff down over itself and the remaining unstuffed foot of the sock until you reach the fiberfill.

fiberfill

sock

Set the base with the pipe-cleaner tentacles inside the top of the stuffed sock so that the tentacles stick out of the top. You can paint your sock base if you wish.

Make the little clownfish on the next page to swim through your sea anemone.

Clownfish Magnet

Here is what you need:

tongue depressor
black permanent marker
cupcake wrapper
orange-colored glue
white glue
white poster paint and a paintbrush
scissors
piece of sticky-backed magnet
Styrofoam tray for drying

The little clownfish has defenses against the deadly sea anemone. It floats with the rhythm of the anemone's tentacles to avoid contact with them—and it secretes a mucous coating that prevents the tentacles from discharging their poison.

Here is what you do:

Break a 2-inch (5-cm) -long piece off each end of the tongue depressor. Use the black marker to draw a fish face on the rounded end and to draw stripes along the body. (If you are making a fish for your sea anemone stabile you will need to draw details on the other stick, too, to make the other side of the fish.)

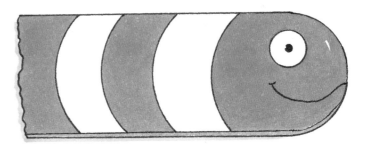

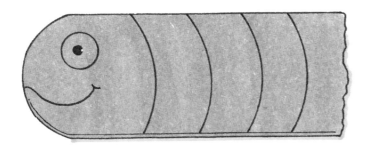

Paint the stripes on the fish white. Color the rest of the fish with a thin coating of orange glue. Let the project dry before continuing.

3 Cut a tail, two bottom and two top fins, and a fin for each side of the fish from the bumpy sides of the cupcake wrapper.

4 Use the black marker to add detail to the fins.

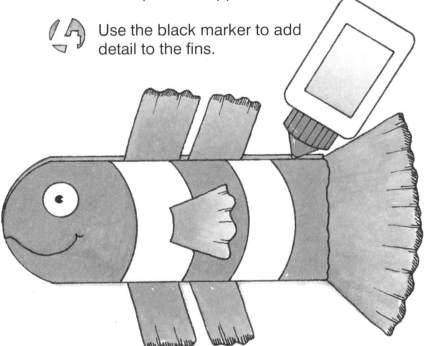

5 Glue the two sticks together with the tail and the top and bottom fins in between. Glue a fin on one or both sides of the fish, depending on whether you are making a magnet or a fish for your sea anemone.

6 Add color to the fins with the orange glue and let the glue dry.

If you made a one-sided fish, press a piece of sticky-backed magnet on the back of the fish and find a refrigerator for the fish to swim across. If you made a fish for your sea anemone stabile, glue the fish swimming among the deadly tentacles!

Angelfish Wall Hanging

Here is what you need:

five or six old neckties
corrugated cardboard
bubble wrap with large bubbles
scrap of black paper
blue poster paint and paintbrush
scissors
hole punch
piece of yarn
white glue

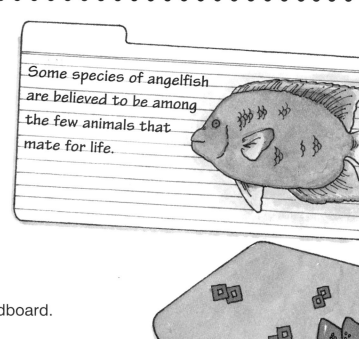

Some species of angelfish are believed to be among the few animals that mate for life.

Here is what you do:

Cut a 15-inch (38-cm) circle from the cardboard.

Paint the cardboard circle blue and let it dry.

To make each fish, cut a 6-inch (15-cm) -long piece from the wide end of a necktie. Round off the cut end of the tie to form the back of the fish. Cut a 2½-inch (6.3-cm) piece from the small end of the same tie or a different one for the tail of the fish. Cut a top and bottom fin on the fold of the tie scraps.

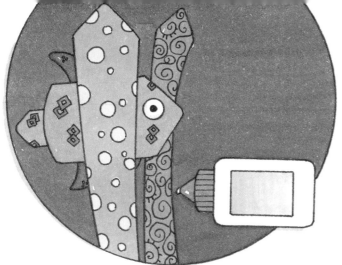

Cut four 10- to 12-inch (25- to 30-cm) pieces of seaweed from the narrow ends of the neckties. If the piece is not an end cut, you will need to cut the piece into a point at one end.

Arrange the seaweed pieces so that they come up from the bottom of the circle. Tuck the angelfish bodies between and behind the seaweed to look like they are swimming through it. Add the tails and fins. When you have an arrangement you like, glue everything in place.

Cut a large bubble out of the bubble wrap for each fish. Cut a pupil from the black paper for each eye. Cut a tiny slit in the back of each bubble and slip a pupil into each eye. Glue an eye on each fish.

Punch a hole in the top of the cardboard. String a piece of yarn through the hole and tie the two ends together to make a hanger.

Hang up these beautiful and unusual fish for all to admire.

Scary Shark Puppet

Here is what you need:

two 42-ounce (1,193-gram) oatmeal boxes
adult-size black or dark-gray sock
black construction paper
two cotton balls
scissors
white glue
masking tape

Here is what you do:

Cut down the side of one of the oatmeal boxes. Cut the rim off the top of the box. Cut out the bottom of the box.

Carefully peel the printed outer layer off the upper portion of the box to expose the gray cardboard underlayer.

Cut 1-inch (2.5-cm) -long pointed teeth all the way around the peeled rim of the box. If you want the teeth to look whiter than the color of the cardboard, you will need to paint them.

Wrap the cut box around itself until the mouth opening is about 4 inches (10 cm) across. Wrap the outside of the box with strips of masking tape to hold the rolled cardboard in place.

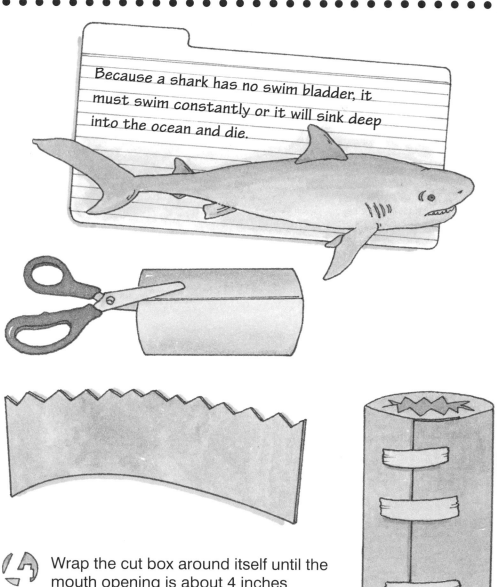

Because a shark has no swim bladder, it must swim constantly or it will sink deep into the ocean and die.

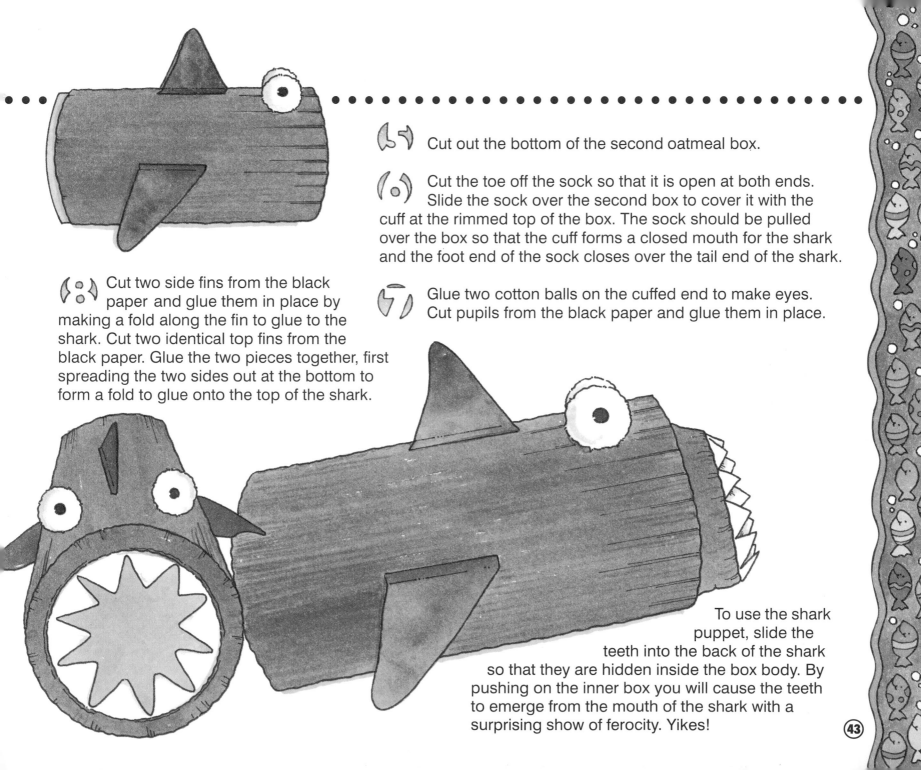

Cut out the bottom of the second oatmeal box.

Cut the toe off the sock so that it is open at both ends. Slide the sock over the second box to cover it with the cuff at the rimmed top of the box. The sock should be pulled over the box so that the cuff forms a closed mouth for the shark and the foot end of the sock closes over the tail end of the shark.

Cut two side fins from the black paper and glue them in place by making a fold along the fin to glue to the shark. Cut two identical top fins from the black paper. Glue the two pieces together, first spreading the two sides out at the bottom to form a fold to glue onto the top of the shark.

Glue two cotton balls on the cuffed end to make eyes. Cut pupils from the black paper and glue them in place.

To use the shark puppet, slide the teeth into the back of the shark so that they are hidden inside the box body. By pushing on the inner box you will cause the teeth to emerge from the mouth of the shark with a surprising show of ferocity. Yikes!

Water-spouting Whale

Here is what you need:

gallon-size plastic milk jug
14½-ounce (435-ml) dish detergent bottle
aluminum foil
black permanent marker
scissors
masking tape

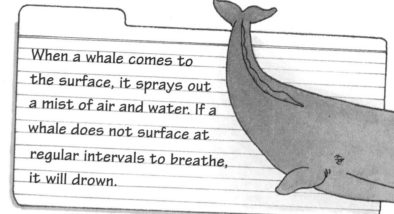

When a whale comes to the surface, it sprays out a mist of air and water. If a whale does not surface at regular intervals to breathe, it will drown.

Here is what you do:

Cut around the entire handle and neck portion of the bottle to remove the top section.

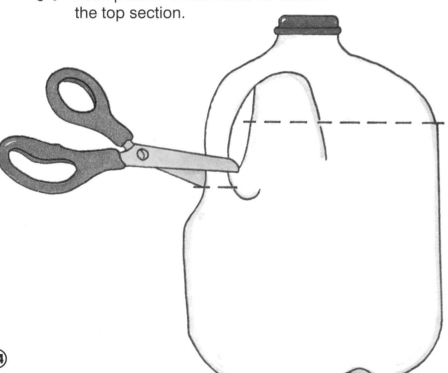

Turn the remaining bottle on its side so that one of the corners is the bottom of the whale body. Cut a small hole in the center of the top corner of the jug for the spout. The detergent bottle should be able to fit inside the whale body with the top of the bottle up through the cut hole.

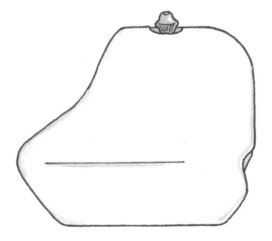

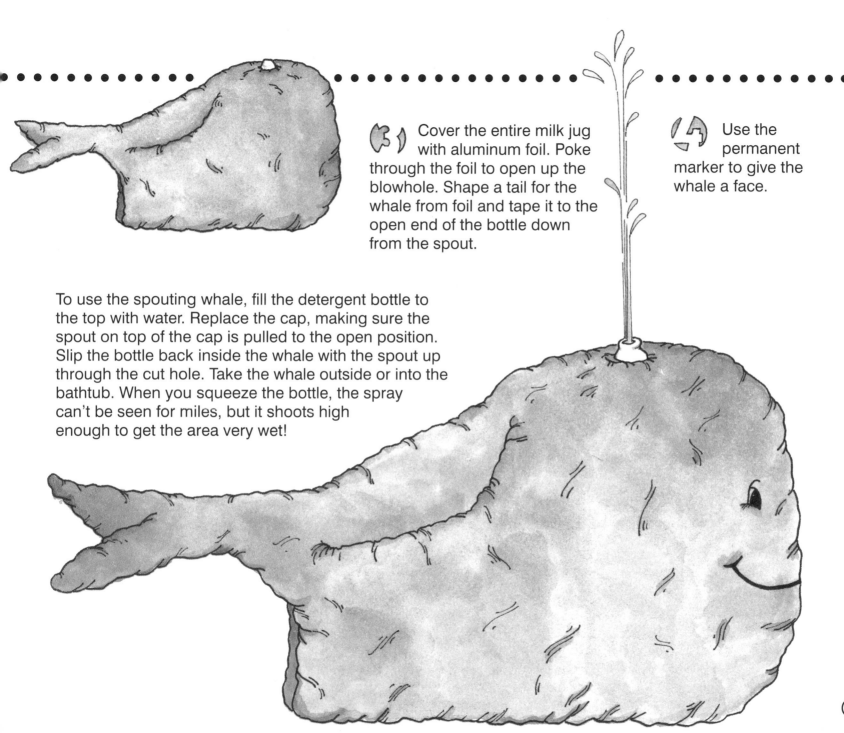

Cover the entire milk jug with aluminum foil. Poke through the foil to open up the blowhole. Shape a tail for the whale from foil and tape it to the open end of the bottle down from the spout.

Use the permanent marker to give the whale a face.

To use the spouting whale, fill the detergent bottle to the top with water. Replace the cap, making sure the spout on top of the cap is pulled to the open position. Slip the bottle back inside the whale with the spout up through the cut hole. Take the whale outside or into the bathtub. When you squeeze the bottle, the spray can't be seen for miles, but it shoots high enough to get the area very wet!

Leaping Dolphin Puppet

Here is what you need:

16-ounce (473-ml) plastic soda bottle
adult-size dark-gray sock
adult-size white sock with very stretchy cuff
blue poster paint and a paintbrush
square tissue box
black permanent marker
fiberfill
white glue
scissors

The jaw line of the bottlenose dolphin makes it look as though it is always smiling!

Here is what you do:

 Cut off the base of the bottle.

 Put the bottle inside the gray sock, spout first, so that the open end of the bottle is at the open end of the sock.

 The seam on top of the toe of the sock forms a mouth for the dolphin. Use the black marker to draw eyes.

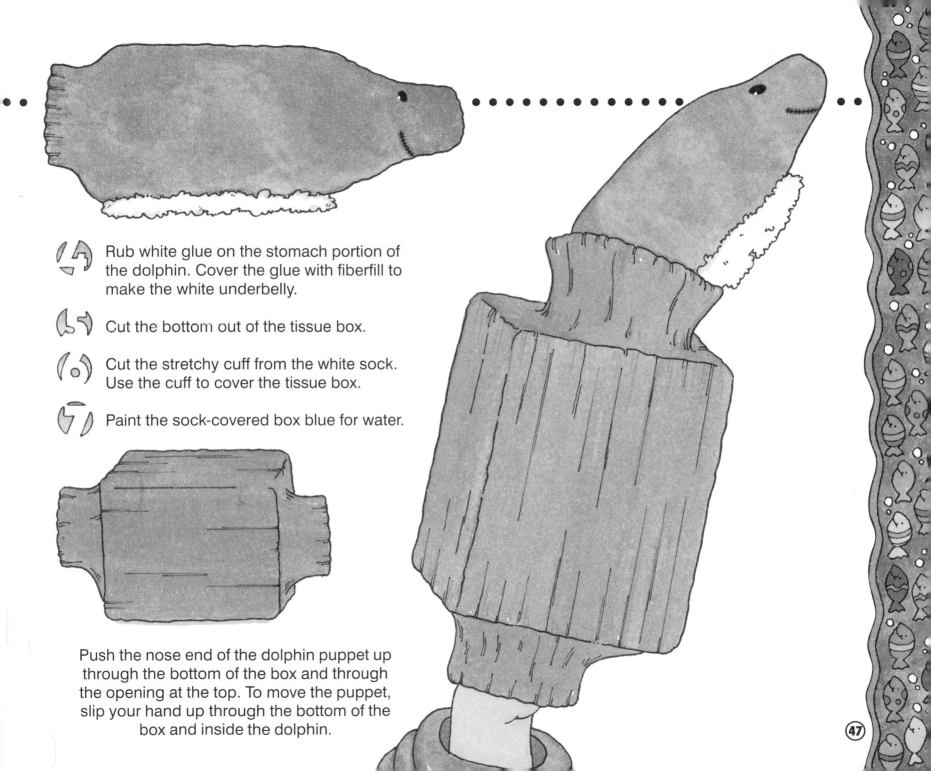

Rub white glue on the stomach portion of the dolphin. Cover the glue with fiberfill to make the white underbelly.

Cut the bottom out of the tissue box.

Cut the stretchy cuff from the white sock. Use the cuff to cover the tissue box.

Paint the sock-covered box blue for water.

Push the nose end of the dolphin puppet up through the bottom of the box and through the opening at the top. To move the puppet, slip your hand up through the bottom of the box and inside the dolphin.

Books About Oceans

Baker, Lucy. *Life in the Oceans.* New York: Franklin Watts, 1990.

Bramwell, Martyn. *The Oceans.* New York: Franklin Watts, 1987.

Carter, Katherine Jones. *Oceans.* Chicago: Childrens Press, 1982.

Cole, Joanna. *The Magic School Bus on the Ocean Floor.* New York: Scholastic, 1992.

Cook, Jan Leslie. *The Mysterious Undersea World*. Washington, D.C.: National Geographic Society, 1980.

Craig, Janet. *What's Under the Ocean?* Mahwah, NJ: Troll, 1982.

Crema, Laura. *Look Inside the Ocean.* New York: Grosset & Dunlap, 1993.

Ganeri, Anita. *The Oceans Atlas.* London; New York: Dorling Kindersley, 1994.

Hoff, Mary King. *Our Endangered Planet.* Minneapolis: Lerner Publications, 1991.

Jennings, Terry. *Oceans and Seas.* Danbury, CT: Grolier Education Corporation, 1992.

Knight, David C. *Let's Find Out About the Ocean.* New York: Franklin Watts, 1970.

Lambert, David. *Seas and Oceans.* Morristown, NJ: Silver Burdett Press, 1988.

MacQuitty, Miranda. *Ocean.* New York: Knopf, 1995.

Morris, Neil. *Oceans.* New York: Crabtree Publishing Co.,1996.

Mudd-Ruth, Maria. *The Ultimate Ocean Book.* New York: Artists & Writers Guild Books/Golden Books/ Western Publishing, 1995.

O'Mara, Anna. *Oceans.* Mankato, MN: Bridgestone Books, 1996.

Sayre, April. *Ocean.* New York: Twenty-First Century Books, 1996.

Talbot, Frank (Editor). *Under the Sea.* Alexandria, VA: Time-Life Books, 1995.

Yardley, Thompson. *Make a Splash.* Brookfield, CT: Millbrook Press, 1992.